STARTING A PETITION

TAKING CIVIC ACTION

I0805194

Spencer Toole

CIVICS FOR THE REAL WORLD™

Rosen Classroom™

Published in 2019 by The Rosen Publishing Group, Inc.
29 East 21st Street, New York, NY 10010

Copyright © 2019 by The Rosen Publishing Group, Inc.

All rights reserved. No part of this book may be reproduced in any form without permission in writing from the publisher, except by a reviewer.

Book Design: Rachel Rising
Editor: Ryan Wolf

Photo Credits: Cover steve estvanik/Shutterstock.com; p. 4 Charles Haire/Shutterstock.com; p. 7 David Tadevosian/Shutterstock.com; p. 8 Uber Images/Shutterstock.com; p. 11 pavla/Shutterstock.com; p. 12 Flash-ka/Shutterstock.com; p. 14 Jaren Jai Wicklund/Shuttterstock.com.

ISBN: 9781538365632
6-pack ISBN: 9781538365649

Manufactured in the United States of America

CPSIA Compliance Information: Batch #WS18RC: For Further Information contact Rosen Publishing, New York, New York at 1-800-237-9932

CONTENTS

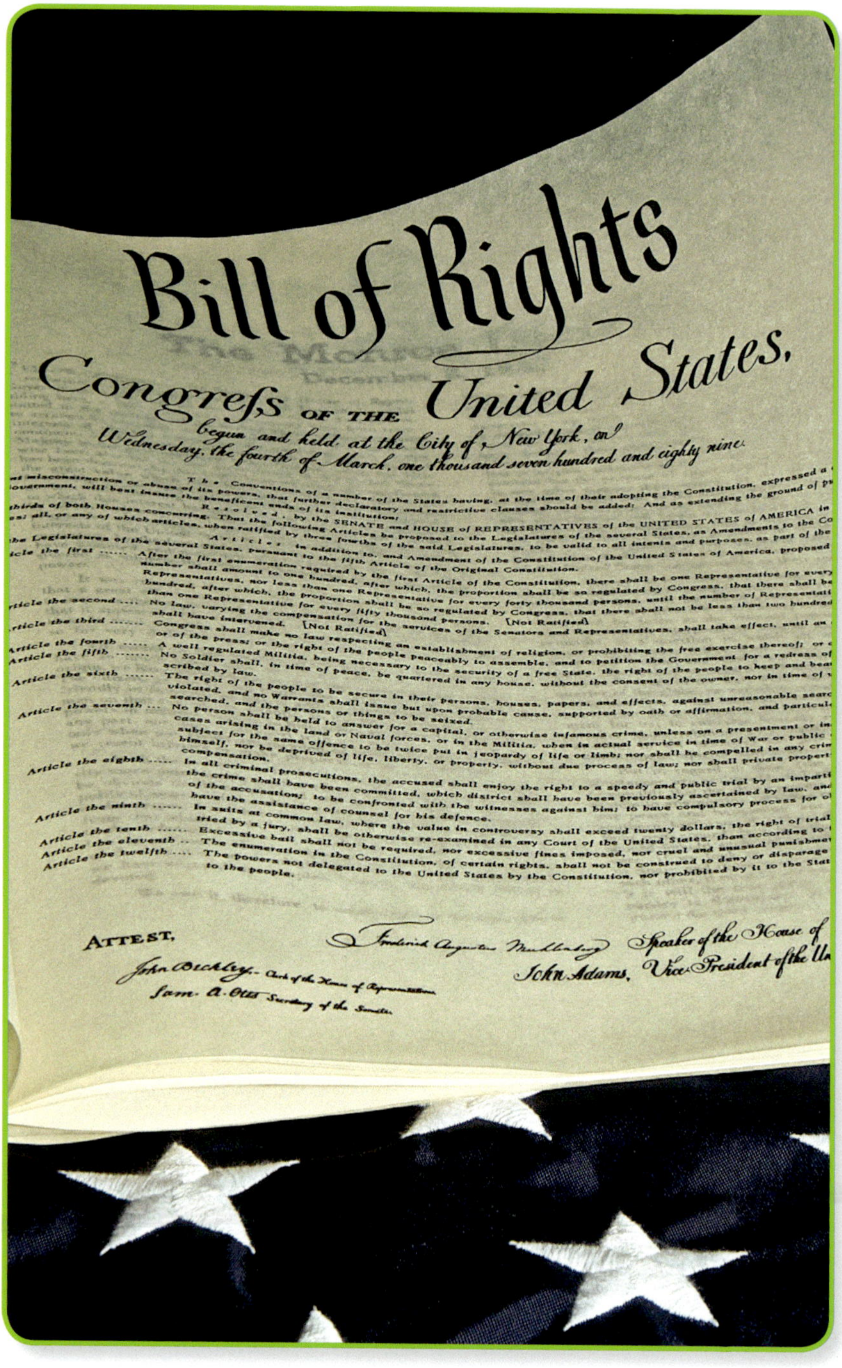
Bill of Rights
Congress of the United States,
begun and held at the City of New York, on
Wednesday, the fourth of March, one thousand seven hundred and eighty nine
ATTEST,
John Adams, Vice President of the Un

AN IMPORTANT RIGHT

The U.S. **Constitution** gives us many rights. One of them, promised in the First Amendment, or change to the Constitution, is the right to "petition the government for a redress of grievances."

This means citizens have the right to ask the government to correct something that's wrong. A petition is also a written **request** asking a person or government to do something. Anyone can start a petition. Even you!

WHAT CAN YOU DO?

What's something you'd like to see corrected in your community? Maybe you'd like playground swings that everyone, including kids with different abilities, can use. Or maybe you think people drive too fast on a street by your school.

You could write a petition addressing these things. You could ask your local government to make the playground more **accessible**. You could ask officials to lower the speed limit on the street.

ELEMENTS OF A PETITION

Many petitions start with a letter to the person or group who can fix the problem. Explain the problem the best you can. Use good manners and be respectful. Use your best writing.

Tell the person or group what you want to change, how that will help, and why it's a good idea. After you've written the letter, you can start getting **signatures** from people who agree with you.

SAFETY FIRST!

You're going to want to get as many people to sign your petition as you can, but you have to be careful. If you want to go door-to-door to ask people to sign, be sure you always have an adult with you.

People now put many petitions online. That way, all you have to do is send people the link to the website so they can sign.

DELIVERED!

Once you've written your petition and collected as many signatures as you can, you must **deliver** it. Sometimes you will mail the petition to officials, especially those from your state or the country. If your petition is online, you can email the link. If the officials are local, you can deliver your petition by hand. You can visit your school building or city, town, or village hall with an adult.

WORKING FOR CHANGE

It might be a while before you get an answer to your petition. Sometimes, you might not get an answer at all. If this happens, ask your officials why or try again! You might not always get the answer you want. Still, it's important to work for change in your community. If no one tries to fix problems or change things that are wrong, nothing will ever get better!

GLOSSARY

accessible: Able to be reached or used.

constitution: The basic laws by which a country, state, or group is governed.

deliver: To take something to a person or place.

request: The act of asking for something in a polite way.

signature: A person's name in that person's writing.

INDEX